A Kid's Guide to
Martial Arts

KUNG FU

功夫

Alix Wood

PowerKiDS
press.

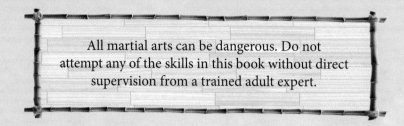

All martial arts can be dangerous. Do not attempt any of the skills in this book without direct supervision from a trained adult expert.

Published in 2013 by The Rosen Publishing Group, Inc.
29 East 21st Street, New York, NY 10010

Copyright © 2013 Alix Wood Books

Editor: Sara Antill
Designer: Alix Wood
Consultant: Sandra Beale-Ellis, National Association of Karate and Martial Art Schools (NAKMAS)

With grateful thanks to Finnian Cooling and everyone at Kernow Martial Arts; James, Joshua, and Elaine Latus, Olivia and Dereka Antonio, Solomon Brown, Ryan Fletcher, Alex Gobbitt, Hayden Hambly, Max Keeling, Joshua Nowell, Kyanna and Katie-Marie Orchard, Natasha Shear, Niamh Stephen, Chris Tanner, Jazmine Watkins, and Emily.

Photo Credits: Cover, 1 © Blue Jean Images/Corbis; 4 © Renato Ganoza; 5, 6, 7, 8 right, 11, 15 center, 18, 19 bottom, 24, 31 © Shutterstock; all other images © Chris Robbins

Library of Congress Cataloging-in-Publication Data

Wood, Alix.
 Kung fu / by Alix Wood.
    p. cm. — (A kid's guide to martial arts)
 Includes index.
 ISBN 978-1-4777-0319-9 (library binding) — ISBN 978-1-4777-0360-1 (pbk.) —
ISBN 978-1-4777-0361-8 (6-pack)
 1. Kung fu—Juvenile literature. I. Title.
 GV1114.7.W67 2013
 796.815'9—dc23

                    2012030865

Manufactured in the United States of America

CPSIA Compliance Information: Batch #: W13PK2: For Further Information contact Rosen Publishing, New York, New York at 1-800-237-9932

Contents

What Is Kung Fu?

*Kung fu is a Chinese martial art. There are several hundred forms of kung fu. All styles teach the use of throws, holds, weapons, and **self-defense**. Some styles **mimic** the movements of animals.*

Early Chinese martial arts were mainly used as exercises to prepare soldiers for battle. An Indian monk named Bodhidharma founded a Buddhist temple called Shaolin. His monks were too weak to **meditate** for long and fell asleep. Bodhidharma created exercises to strengthen them, and this became Shaolin kung fu. When the monks defeated temple invaders, they bcame famous for their fighting skills.

A statue of a monk outside the Shaolin temple, home of kung fu

The monks were seen as a threat to invading Manchurians, who burned the temple. The survivors fled to different parts of southeast Asia and set up new schools. Each school's style became a little different. That's how we ended up with so many different types of kung fu.

A wushu demonstration

The ancient Chinese symbol of yin and yang (above) is often used as a symbol of tai chi, a form of kung fu. Its design shows two opposite forces working together. In kung fu, strength and gentleness are the opposite forces.

HARD WORK

In Chinese, "kung fu" means "hard work." Only recently has "kung fu" been used to mean a martial art. In Chinese "wushu" means "martial art," but the sport of wushu is a **noncombat** demonstration sport, and the sport of kung fu is a martial art! How confusing!

History and Styles

*Many kung fu styles have developed, each with their own set of **techniques**. Some styles are similar and are often grouped together as "families" or "schools."*

Some styles mimic animal movements, and others are inspired by Chinese myths and legends. Some styles concentrate on harnessing **qi**, while others concentrate on competition. Chinese martial arts are often split into northern and southern styles, depending on whether they started north or south of the Yangtze River. Northern styles tend to have fast, powerful kicks, high jumps, and flowing, quick moves. Southern styles have strong arm and hand techniques, stable **stances**, and fast footwork.

CHINA   Beijing •

Yangtze River

Map of China

Wing chun is a southern style, and the style that actor Bruce Lee practiced. It is one of the most popular forms of kung fu, and was invented by a woman. Yim Wing-chun turned down a marriage proposal, saying she'd reconsider if the man could beat her in a martial art match. She learned a new martial art from a friend, and then beat her suitor.

Statue of Bruce Lee on the Avenue of Stars, in Hong Kong

QI

"Qi" means "life energy." The development of qi is important in many martial arts. Meditation makes you mentally ready to try what seems to be physically impossible.

Kung fu trains both the "internal" and the "external." The external is the hands, the eyes, the body, and stances. The internal is the heart, the spirit, the mind, breathing, and strength.

7

Kung Fu Equipment

The clothes you will need depend on your school. If there is a uniform, the shool will usually sell it. For your first session, try wearing sneakers, loose cotton drawstring pants, and a T-shirt.

There is no strict kung fu uniform. Some people wear a traditional satin jacket with a **mandarin collar** and ornamental buttons and loose satin pants. Some clubs are more casual and wear T-shirts and sweatpants, perhaps with a satin kung fu sash. It's best to check with your club before you buy any clothes.

Kung fu sash

Traditional satin jacket and pants

How to tie a kung fu sash

1 Find the center of the sash and place it on the center of your stomach.

2 Pull the right end of the sash around your body so that you have a long end on the right and a short end on the left.

3 Tie the two ends in a secure single knot, like the knot when you are tying your shoe.

4 Take the longer end and pull it up into a half bow. Wrap the other end around the half bow and pull it through and down. It's like tying your shoe except you make one loop instead of two.

5 Fold down the bow so that it is neat and out of the way. Smooth out any creases in the sash until it is as wide as possible.

LEFT, RIGHT, OR CENTER?

In some schools, if you are a student you tie the knot on your left hip. An assistant instructor ties it on the right hip. Instructors tie it in the center. In other schools, boys tie it on the left and girls on the right.

Kung Fu School

Your kung fu school may be a multipurpose hall, or it may be a specially-built martial arts school. Either way, there will be rules you will need to follow and customs you will need to learn.

Your school may have a picture or statue of a Chinese man with a red face. This is General Guan, patron saint of martial arts and justice. Kung fu schools honor Guan Yu, not just because he was strong in battle. He was modest, and treated friend and enemy alike with honor and respect. He used the minimum force necessary to get the job done.

A statue of General Guan displayed at a kung fu school

You will need to learn the kung fu **salute**, shown below. The fist is the Sun and the open palm is the Moon. The salute shows respect toward your instructor, your fellow pupils, and to kung fu. You perform the salute at the start and end of your session, and when starting or ending an exercise.

The standing salute

Stand with heels together and toes slightly apart. Put you right open hand over your left clenched fist (left). Then wrap your open hand around the fist and bow from the waist. Hold your hands at nose height. The command for making the salute is "Yu pei." "Yu" means "ready with the body," and "pei" means "ready with the mind."

Unlike some other martial arts, in kung fu you always keep your eyes fixed on the person you are saluting.

Warming Up

It is important to warm up before you start your kung fu session. This will stop you from pulling muscles. Here are some good exercises you can use for your warm-up.

Remember, if you feel any pain, stop what you are doing and move onto a different exercise or stretch.

Hip twists

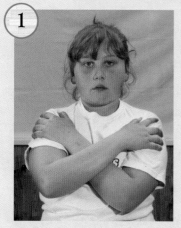

1

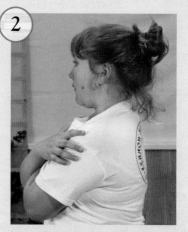

2

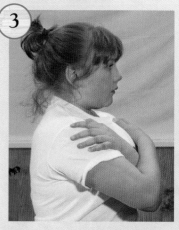

3

Cross your arms in front of you and hold your opposite shoulders. Bend your knees slightly to stop them from twisting.

Keeping your elbows tightly at your sides, begin to turn from your hips to one side.

Then turn from your hips to the other side. Begin slowly and do as many as you can.

Butterfly stretch

1

Sit down with the soles of your feet pressed together. Hold onto your toes.

2

Lean forward, pulling slightly. Hold, then pull your feet in a little closer and repeat.

Wrist exercises

1

Place your palms together. Gently press in and down, hold for 10 seonds.

2

Raise your elbows, and put the backs of your hands together. Press and hold for 10 seconds.

Flexibility is an important part of kung fu, but remember, if you try any of these exercises at home, always stretch gradually and carefully.

Stances

A stance is a way of standing. If your stance is solid, your moves have a strong, stable base. Different stances are useful for different moves. Practice holding these for a few seconds each.

Try making your feet match the drawings. The red line going across is where your shoulders should be, over your feet.

Forward stance

Horse stance

Stand with your feet wide apart, turned slightly inward. Sit low with your back straight.

Lean forward on your front leg, with your rear leg straight. Your front foot points forward, with your rear foot turned out a little.

Either hold your hands in fists, or try some of the hand techniques on the next pages. This girl is doing a crane's beak and a willow leaf palm.

Crane stance

Cross stance

Tiger stance

From a horse stance, slide one leg behind the other so the kneecap touches the inside of the other knee. Rest on the toe of the rear leg.

Raise your front leg until your toe almost touches your other knee. Point your toe toward the ground. Your other leg should be straight but not locked.

Start from a forward stance, then sit back until you weight is over your back leg. Bring your front leg back and slightly to the side, with your heel off the floor.

15

Hands and Gates

In kung fu, the body is split into six gates. Gates are different zones you protect if you're defending or strike if you're attacking. Learn these kung fu hand techniques to fill your zones or to strike an opponent.

The six gates are upper, middle, and lower body, and left and right sides. If a zone is attacked, simply fill the space in that zone. It doesn't matter what the attack is, only which zone it's coming to. Kung fu uses the idea that no two objects can be in the same space at the same time. Filling space is not the same as blocking. If a punch is stronger than a block, then the punch will win. Filling space avoids contests of strength but still stops a strike.

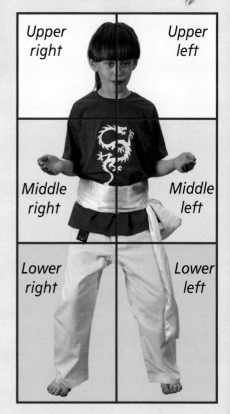

The six gates

THE SIX GATES

The upper two gates are called the "heaven" gates, the middle two are called the "man" gates, and the lower two are called the "earth" gates.

Willow leaf palm

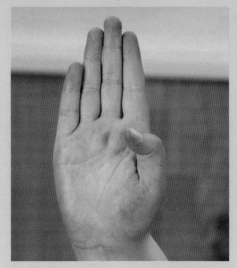

The willow leaf palm can be used in five ways. The inside and outside edges can be used to strike. The back of the hand can strike, too. The heel of the hand or the palm can be used to thrust.

Horizontal Fist

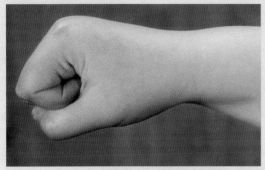

For a kung fu fist, close your four fingers into your palm. Don't clench your fist. The knuckles should form a flat surface. Fold your thumb over your fingers. Keep your wrist straight.

Eagle claw

To do an eagle claw, bend your fingers and thumb. Keep your fingers together and bend the wrist back. Hold the thumb to the side. An eagle claw is very useful for gripping.

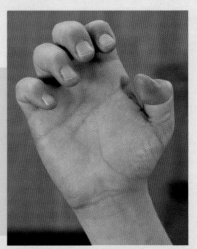

17

Strikes

*Strikes are an important part of kung fu. You can use the fingertips, wrists, **forearms**, shoulders, back, and hips to strike an opponent as well as the more usual fists, palms, elbows, knees, and feet.*

When performing fist strikes it is important to strike using a safe part of your hand. Use the simple rules below, too, to avoid hurting yourself.

Strike with these two knuckles.

HARD AND SOFT

Remember these simple rules when striking an opponent.

- Hard can hit soft
- Hard can't hit hard
- Soft can hit soft
- Soft can hit hard

So, don't use your knuckles to strike a bony area. You'll hurt your hand. Use a soft area like your palm.

Single palm strike

Palm strikes hit with the bottom part of the palm, where the hand meets the wrist. A palm strike has just as much force as a closed fist when done properly with far less risk of injury to the striker's own hand.

Double palm strike

Double palm strikes are done the same way as a single palm strike. Throw your hands forward together, using your palms as the striking surface.

Palm strikes can go up, straight, or down. The most popular palm strike is upward to the chin. This strike pushes your opponent's jaw shut and their head back. It also allows you to get a second strike in as your opponent won't be able to see you.

Blocks

A block is a way of stopping a strike from hitting you. In kung fu, blocks tend to be done close to your body. This means your attackers have to use up their energy coming to you.

There are four basic blocking areas—up, down, in, and out. The hand doesn't make a fist, but is relaxed. Kung fu teaches that you get the most power and speed if you tense up just at the last second. A tense arm is slower through a swing. This is true for strikes and blocks.

Outward block

Use the outside of your wrist, hand, or forearm to push the attack away. Guard your body with your other arm at the same time.

Inward block

Press the inside of your wrist against the attacker's arm. Make contact and then twist your hips and push the strike to the side.

Downward block

A downward block needs timing. Let your arm fall to block the strike. Protect your body and face with the other arm.

Upward block

Raise your arm up underneath the arm of your attacker. Protect your body with your other arm.

Choke block

A choke block is useful if you are close to your attacker. As she throws a strike, move toward, rather than away, from her.

Slam your hand against the inside of her attacking shoulder. This "chokes" the energy out of her strike.

Kicks

There are differences in the types of kicks used in different styles of kung fu. Southern styles use low kicks. Northern styles do higher kicks. The whirling spin kicks are typical of the northern stye.

STRIKES

Use one of these areas of your foot when you kick.

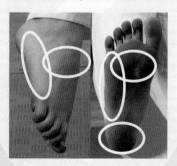

Front snap kick

Lift the knee of the kicking leg, and bring the lower leg forward.

Snap your foot out. Swing out from your knee not your hip. Bring your leg back quickly.

Low kick

Snap your leg out just like a front snap kick, but aim lower.

Side kick

Raise one knee and strike out to the side. Strike with the outer edge of your foot.

Heel kick

With your toes back, thrust your heel at the target while straightening your non-kicking leg.

Back kick

Try a spin back kick. Face your opponent and lift up one knee. Spin around on the other foot by pushing your hip around and then aim the kick behind you.

You can use a kick to block an incoming kick, too. These are called check kicks.

Aim at or below the waist with this back kick.

23

Meditation

*In kung fu, meditation is an important part of basic training. Meditation can be used to develop **focus** and the ability to think quickly and clearly. Meditation is the basis for qi training, called qigong.*

The ability to perform extraordinary feats, like withstanding heavy strikes and breaking hard objects, is said to come down to qigong training. Breathing and meditation are a big part of martial arts. Through these you are able to control and connect your body and mind. During meditation your breathing slows down. This makes you relaxed and less anxious.

Sit with your legs crossed, your eyes closed, and your hands held like this. This position is called shuni mudra and makes you patient and brave. The middle finger and thumb lightly touch at the tips. The other fingers are held out gently.

The five aims of kung fu meditation

- Meditation develops a strong mind.
- A strong mind develops concentration.
- Concentration brings control.
- Control develops discipline.
- Discipline brings self-discipline.

DEATH TOUCH

Some kung fu styles believe in focusing qi into a single point on your opponent's body when attacking. This technique is known as *dim mak*, or the death touch. Some people believe the kung fu actor Bruce Lee's early death may have been due to a dim mak strike he received weeks before he died.

Deep breathing and *dan tian*

There are three dan tian areas. The important one for deep breathing is the lower one. It is three finger widths below the **navel** and a couple of inches back inside the body.

Upper dan tian, or "third eye"

Middle dan tian

Lower dan tian

1. Breathe in and out through your nose. Do one big long breath out to clear the lungs.

2. Breathe in down to the lower dan tian so your belly expands. Repeat steps 1 and 2. Imagine a golden ball of energy growing in your lower dan tian. With each breath this light grows brighter.

Forms and Styles

In kung fu, some styles resemble animals' hunting styles. The Shaolin five animals are dragon, tiger, snake, crane, and leopard. Each provide different techniques for attacking and defending.

These five animals are mainly seen in southern styles of kung fu. There are animals in other styles, for instance praying mantis, deer, monkey, and bear styles.

Tiger claw

King of all land beasts, the tiger style is simple and powerful. The main target is the opponent's throat. A strong back and neck are essential. The main technique is the tiger claw.

This girl is doing a tiger claw.

Snake hand

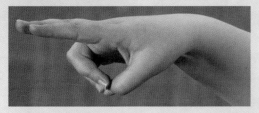

The snake form uses quick, piercing strikes. There are no closed fists in the snake form. The hands are used for chops and finger strikes.

Leopard fist

The leopard form is a fast, powerful style with relaxed, whiplike techniques. You need to be flexible and fast.

Dragon claw

The dragon form uses **circular** movements and sudden strikes. The claw is the main hand technique. The moves use the waist in a powerful whipping action.

Crane's beak

Crane style movements are circular like wing movements. The strikes are soft and relaxed, but with speed and force. The crane form uses a "beak" to strike targets.

NORTHERN STYLES

"Praying Mantis" is one of the best known northern styles of kung fu. The style uses whiplike circular actions. The hand is made into a hook shape.

Kung Fu Language

China has two main languages, Mandarin and Cantonese. Some kung fu southern styles speak Cantonese. Northern styles speak Mandarin. Mandarin is the official language of China, and most Cantonese speakers will at least understand Mandarin.

Pinyin is the name for the official way to write Mandarin sounds into our alphabet. It was invented in the 1950s. An older system was used in the first half of the 20th century. The Mandarin script for kung fu was **romanized** as "kung fu" in the old system, but "gong fu" in Pinyin. You will find some people spell it "gong fu" now.

The top symbol "kung" or "gong" means "work" and the bottom symbol "fu" means "man."

work

man

Chinese symbols for kung fu

28

One of the times you may hear Chinese at your kung fu class is when your instructor is counting.

Counting to 10

English	Mandarin	Symbol	English	Mandarin	Symbol
one	yi	一	six	liu	六
two	er	二	seven	qi	七
three	san	三	eight	ba	八
four	si	四	nine	jiu	九
five	wu	五	ten	shi	十

Kung fu words you may hear

Mandarin	How to say it	What it means
sifu	*sure foo*	instructor
todai	*toodee*	pupil
si-gung	*shr gung*	sifu's teacher
si-tai-gung	*shr tie gung*	si-gung's teacher
si-jo	*shr joe*	si-tai-gung's teacher
sanda	*sanda*	sparring
kow tow	*kow tow*	bow
gen lai	*gun lie*	salute

Glossary

circular (SER-kyuh-ler)
Having the form of a circle.

focus (FOH-kis)
Concentration.

forearms (FOR-armz)
The part of human arms
between the elbow and
the wrist.

mandarin collar
(MAN-duh-rin KAH-ler)
A short, unfolded stand-up
collar style on a shirt
or jacket.

meditate (MEH-dih-tayt)
To train the mind to get a
level of inner thought which
gives someone some benefit.

mimic (MIH-mik)
To imitate closely.

navel (NAY-vul)
The indentation in the
middle of the abdomen
where the umbilical cord
was attached.

noncombat
(nahn-KOM-bat)
Not including or
requiring combat.

qi (CHEE)
The life force whose
existence and properties
are the basis of much
Chinese philosophy
and medicine.

romanized
(ROH-muh-nyzd)
Translated into the
Roman alphabet.

salute (sah-LOOT)
To greet with a respectful bow
or hand gesture.

self-defense
(self-dih-FENS)
The act of defending oneself.

techniques (tek-NEEKS)
The ways in which physical
movements are used.

stances (STANS-es)
Ways of standing.

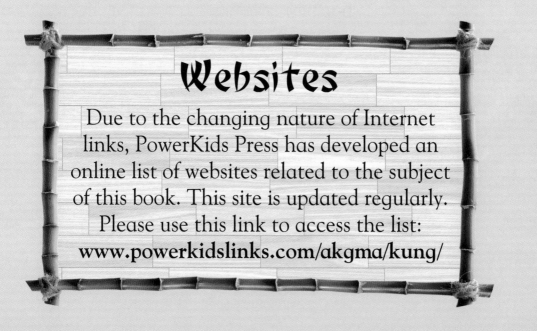

Websites

Due to the changing nature of Internet
links, PowerKids Press has developed an
online list of websites related to the subject
of this book. This site is updated regularly.
Please use this link to access the list:
www.powerkidslinks.com/akgma/kung/

Read More

Eng, Paul. *Kungfu for Kids.* Martial Arts for Kids. North Clarendon, VT: Tuttle Publishing, 2005.

Ollhoff, Jim. *Kung Fu.* World of Martial Arts. Minneapolis, MN: ABDO & Daughters, 2008.

Olson, Stuart Alve. *Tai Chi for Kids: Move with the Animals.* Rochester, VT: Bear Cub Books, 2001.

Index